T0123623

Priceless Stones
and
Endless Ripples

LeVerta Massey

WESTBOW
PRESS®
A DIVISION OF THOMAS NELSON
& ZONDERVAN

WestBow Press books may be ordered through booksellers or by contacting:

WestBow Press
A Division of Thomas Nelson & Zondervan
1663 Liberty Drive
Bloomington, IN 47403
www.westbowpress.com
1 (866) 928-1240

ISBN: 978-1-9736-7717-8 (sc)
ISBN: 978-1-9736-7719-2 (hc)
ISBN: 978-1-9736-7718-5 (e)

Library of Congress Control Number: 2019916450

Print information available on the last page.

WestBow Press rev. date: 10/21/2019

A priceless stone was cast alone into a dismal sea,
Its ripples ever swelling, rolling, breaking,
Reaching, changing the rocky shore.
A brilliant stone was hurled into a murky sea,
Its ripples ever swelling, rolling, breaking,
Reaching, breaking the stony ground,
transforming the minds of men.
A gem of inestimable value has become the chief cornerstone,
A smooth stone, the rock of ages, the rock of our salvation,
A tried stone, a stone causing ripples ever swelling, rolling,
Breaking, reaching, changing the hearts of men.

by LeVerta Massey

CONTENTS

Book 3: Faith in God Is A Priceless Stone

Book 4: The Peace of God: A Priceless Stone

Book 5: Kindness Is a Priceless Stone

Book 6: Grace Is a Priceless Stone

FOREWORD

I am honored and humbled by the request to write the foreword for LeVerta Massey's publication, *Priceless Stones and Endless Ripples*, because the title itself eloquently speaks to the friendship we shared over many years now. Beyond authoring this book, LeVerta Massey has authored entire chapters of exemplary "lived" faith in my life experiences as a minister, teacher of the gospel, mother, sister, and friend. Her wisdom has left ripples that both challenged and soothed me into spiritual maturity. Her work as an evangelist, teacher, and preacher provided a perpetual quarry of stones from which, and with which, I fortified myself through grief, setbacks, and even blessed promotions. I am excited for those who will read this book. I rejoice in advance for the fortification that will ensue. I rejoice for the enduring ripples of grace that will wash over the reader's soul, leaving no measurable edge or end in time. Thank you, LeVerta, for your obedience in sharing this treasure.

—Rev. Dr. Sheryl L. W. Barnes

PREFACE

One late spring afternoon, I was sitting on the patio, looking out over the small manmade lake behind my home. I noticed that several little children were tossing rocks into the water. Ordinarily, I wouldn't have noticed this, except the Holy Spirit called my attention to the rocks hitting the water and how each rock caused ripples to go out in a seemingly endless pattern.

"What does it mean?" I asked after a while of contemplation.

The Holy Spirit very quietly answered me and said, "That's what personal evangelism is." Every stone tossed into that muddy lake was the love of God being cast out by His people. Each ripple represented the effect the love, kindness, compassion, faithfulness, peace, and grace of God had on this sin-filled world. The ripples went out further and further.

You never know just whose life will be touched by the stones you toss. Every time you touch a life through your testimony or conduct, that touch has a ripple effect. You touch a life today, and that life touches another life, and so on and on it goes.

INTRODUCTION

Then he took his staff in his hand, chose five
smooth stones from the stream, put them in the
pouch of his shepherd's bag and, with his sling
in his hand, approached the Philistine.
—1 Samuel 17:40

The word for *chose* in this passage of scripture is *bachar*, which means David made a careful, well-thought-out choice in selecting those five smooth stones. Only one stone was required to bring down Goliath. The stones you throw into the murky water, which is someone's life, will produce ripples that have eternal consequences.

I remember witnessing to a man at work, who was in a backslidden condition. He received the word God had for him and rededicated his life to the Lord right at work. He returned to his boyhood church and began using his musical gifts for the Lord; as a result he has drawn his granddaughter. His returning to God also caused another man to return, and he has brought his young son to the Lord. The apostle Paul said, "I planted the seed, Apollos watered it, but God made it grow. So, neither he who plants nor he who waters is anything, but only God who makes things grow" (1 Corinthians 3:6–7 NIV).

God can and will use you to plant and cultivate, but remember, it is God who gives the increase. He alone deserves the glory, honor, and all the praise.

Don't Worry about the Return on Your Investment

I warn you; the adversary will try to tell you all your efforts to reach lost souls are useless. Intercessory prayer for one who is sinning must triumph. God says so! The will of the man prayed for doesn't come into question at all. The sinner's connection to God is by fervent intercession. Intercession brings about redemption, and *God gives life through the shed blood of Jesus Christ.* You won't always see immediate results. Sometimes you will invest hours and days of your time, and an individual will turn away and seem not to hear a word you've said. Continue to walk in the truth. Continue to intercede for him or her. Continue to love him or her. Never stop. It's normal for us to be impatient when a soul is at stake. We have tasted and seen that the Lord is good. We know what God has done for us and want to share God's grace with all people.

I labored in prison ministry for over twenty-five years, and there have been times of deep frustration because every week it seemed that the same women and men came to the altar for prayer or salvation during every service. I prayed and sought God for a long time because it looked like nothing was changing. It appeared that all our work had been in vain. It was during this time of despair and discouragement that the Holy Spirit encouraged my heart by letting me know it's more important to hear God say, "Well done," than to receive the praise of men or to feel a sense of pride over how many came to Christ. The glory belongs to God and Him alone. Never forget that winning a soul for the kingdom of God *isn't about you; it's about God!*

This book gives real-life examples of personal evangelism. The stones you will learn to cast are love, compassion, faithfulness, peace, kindness, and grace. The questions and reflections at the end of each chapter are for your study and encouragement. How would you deal with the real-life scenarios (giants) presented in this book? Like David, will you choose the right stone?

Finally, every time you witness, every time you allow God to use you to win a soul for His kingdom, you are casting a stone. Choose your words and actions (stones) carefully—that is, prayerfully—and hurl them by the power and direction of the Holy Spirit, and you will see giants fall and lives forever transformed by the gospel of Jesus Christ (the word alive in you) and God's awesome grace.

This book is dedicated to my wonderful family, without whose love and prayers I couldn't make it. Thank you Debra, Ted, and Lena! I also thank my Pastor, Willie J. Powell and wife, Geraldine, and Grace Fellowship family for their love and support.

LeVerta Massey
Teacher and Evangelist

BOOK 1

Love without Measure
Is a Priceless Stone

CHAPTER 1

God's Lavish Love

How *great* is the *love* the Father has lavished on
us, that we should be called children of God!
—1 John 3:1 (emphasis added)

And he has given us this command: Whoever
loves God must also *love* his brother.
—1 John 4:21 (emphasis added)

How awesome it is to know that the most powerful being in the universe loves you! When you were dead in trespasses and sin, His heart's desire was to save you. He went further than to desire your salvation; He provided the perfect sacrifice after all else had failed: Jesus! "For God so *loved* the world, that He gave His one and only Son, that *whoever* believes in Him shall not perish but have eternal life" (John 3:16, emphasis added).

It's not enough to witness to people and give them our testimony. Hurting people need to *see* God's love. Acts of charity are wonderful, but empty acts of charity aren't enough either. God's love can be felt. It is tangible. Love changes the landscape of a person's life. Love can cause what was dead to rise to new life. God loved us just as we were.

We had nothing to offer Him in exchange for what He offered us. No bargaining chips.

God made *love* a verb when He gave His only begotten Son.

Light on the Word

When we were kids, my little sister made a bologna sandwich with so much mayonnaise that it oozed onto her clothes or whatever happened to be in its path. Similarly, God also generously lavishes His great love on us, so much so that it should ooze from us and affect the lives of everyone with whom we come in contact. People ought to know whose we are by the aroma of love all around us. Christ said, "By this, all men will know that you are my disciples if you *love* one another" (John 13:35, emphasis added).

Read and respond to the following questions:

1. How does knowing how much God loves you affect how you demonstrate love to others?
2. How difficult is it for you to show God's love to strangers?
3. Do your loving ways identify you as a disciple of Christ?

CHAPTER 2

God's Unconditional Love

Let's look further:

> Now a man named Lazarus was sick. He was from Bethany, the village of Mary and her sister Martha. This Mary, whose brother Lazarus now lay sick, was the same one who poured perfume on the Lord and wiped his feet with her hair. So, the sisters sent word to Jesus, "Lord, the one you *love* is sick." When he heard this, Jesus said, "This sickness will not end in death. No, it is for God's glory so that God's Son may be glorified through it." Jesus *loved* Martha and her sister and Lazarus. (John 11:1–5, emphasis added)

Jesus tarried where He was for two more days.

Then he said to his disciples, "Let us go back to Judea."

"But Rabbi," they said, "a short while ago the Jews tried to stone you, and yet you are going back there?" (John 11:7–8)

Authentic love will make things happen. Jesus knew He was taking a chance by going back to the hostile environment He had just left. He knew the hearts and minds of the men who wanted Him dead. Jesus had just told them they weren't His sheep and left them standing there, holding their stones. But His desire to bring glory to the Father and His love for his friend Lazarus compelled Him to return in spite of the danger. The deep sorrow of Mary and Martha caused Jesus to be moved in His spirit and be troubled.

"Where have you laid him?" he asked.

"Come and see, Lord," they replied.

Jesus wept.

Then the Jews said, "See how he *loved* him!" (John 11:34–36, emphasis added)

Whatever the reason for Jesus's tears, whether grief over His friend or over the faithlessness of the people around Him, clearly Jesus was touched by human suffering and pain. The fact that our magnificent Lord wasn't passive or unmoved by the death of His friend should encourage us to love Him and our fellow human beings more. Jesus didn't *tell* us only that we should weep with those who weep and rejoice with those who rejoice; He demonstrated His own words.

This same love (agape) or unconditional love is what we should feel for our friends, relatives, and total strangers. The thought that they might die in their sins should cause us to weep before the throne of God for them. We should be *moved in our spirits* and troubled when our family members, coworkers, and friends don't have a personal relationship with Jesus.

The Jews said, "*See* how he *loved* him!" (emphasis added). The world should be able to see the love of God in our lives. That love is what compels men to desire a relationship with our Savior. Love is what compelled God to desire a relationship with us. Cast this stone into someone's life today and watch the ripples that keep going and going. You will see how God's love will transform a bleak and dismal life into the abundant life Jesus spoke of in John 10:10; this is a life filled with hope and joy that comes from a deep relationship with our Creator. John repeatedly told us God is love. In 1 John 4:20, he wrote, "If anyone says, 'I love God,' yet hates his brother, he is a liar. For anyone who does not love his brother, whom he has seen, cannot love God whom he has not seen." This passage speaks of a personal love relationship between people, not just a spiritual one with God.

Our love for one another represents God. Love isn't selfish. Love isn't proud. Love doesn't seek revenge.

Light on the Word

John stressed that we have a God who cares. This portrait is in stark contrast with an ancient concept of God (without emotions or empathy for humans) that was popular in John's time. Many of Jesus's emotions are revealed in Lazarus's story—compassion, sorrow, indignation, and even mild frustration. Jesus often expressed deep emotion, and since He already knows how we feel, we don't need to fear revealing our true feelings to Him. He understands them because He experienced those same feelings. Remember, Hebrews 4:15 says, "For we do not have a high priest who is unable to sympathize with our weaknesses, but we have one who has been tempted in every way, just as we are—yet was without sin." Be honest and don't try to hide anything from your Savior. He loves you and cares for you.

Consider the following questions and respond:

1. What does God's perfect love do for us, according to 1 John 4:18?
2. According to 1 John 5:3, what is evidence of our love for God?
3. Jesus put His life on the line for the people He loved. How can we demonstrate this kind of self-sacrificing love?

Where Love is, God is.

—Rev. Prof. Henry Drummond

CHAPTER 3

God's Sacrificial Love

Love one another as I have loved you.
Greater love has no one than this than to
lay down one's life for his friends.
—John 15:12–13

Jesus is referring to sacrificial love. It is the kind of love that prefers your sister or brother over yourself and that places more importance on the needs of your neighbor than on your own needs.

I remember experiencing this kind of love from a neighbor I didn't even know. In 2008 I became ill with pneumonia and had to be home for a month and a half. I was too ill to drive to pick up medications and too weak even to prepare a bowl of soup. My neighbor noticed not seeing me leave for work in several days, so she came over to check on me. Unless hospitalized, I had never been treated with such love and kindness from a stranger. She made sure my prescriptions were filled and came over every day for a month to prepare soup for me. Then she enlisted another neighbor to walk my dog. She called my kids to keep them informed of my progress since they weren't able to be around every day.

Over the past few years, I've found out how much she truly loves God. She is a delight to be around. She has an infectious spirit. God's love is evident in her everyday life. I know her sacrifice of coming to my home to serve was an inconvenience. I learned later on that her oldest grandson was suffering from a malignant brain tumor and had only months to live. Even in her own looming personal tragedy, she made time to show the love of God.

Perhaps you won't be required to give your life as Jesus did. Maybe your sacrifice will be giving your time to listen to a friend with a broken heart or a wounded spirit, or to comfort a frantic child. This kind of giving love is often spontaneous, unexpected, and unplanned but reveals the true condition of one's heart.

Sacrificial love will cost you something valuable.

1.   What ways can you think of to practice sacrificial love?
2.   What are you willing to give up to serve others?

Love does not seek her own,
And so, He chose not to stay in heaven's bliss.
Instead He chose a manger, a cross, and a grave
To keep me from being sin's slave.

—LeVerta Massey

CHAPTER 4

Do Everything in Love

Do everything in love.

—1 Corinthians 16:14

Four very simple words: Do everything in love.

Why is it important to do everything in love? Paul felt it necessary to repeat what had already been spoken in 1 Corinthians 13:1–13. It can never be spoken too much because without love, all our noble efforts will seem like nothing more than annoying noise.

"If I speak in the tongues of men and of angels, but have not love, I am only a resounding gong or a clanging cymbal" (1 Corinthians 13:1). Love is what gives my gift, talent, or ability real meaning.

A teacher who teaches with love will go the extra mile to make sure his or her students "get it." Teaching becomes a labor of love, not just a means to earn a paycheck.

I have a dear friend who teaches sophomore and junior English. She spends hours looking for ways to incite her students to learn. She even spends days in the summer painting and decorating her classroom in bright, attractive colors to cut down on the boredom factor with her "kids," as she calls them. Her love for teaching has caused her to be innovative and excited about how her students learn.

Love has overridden complacency and disinterest. As a result, her students always rank high on placement exams. Real love changes outcomes.

The pastor who ministers the word of God with love listens carefully to what God wants to say and applies what he hears with love and tender care. His passion for souls will cause him to deliver the message with passion and deeply desire every convert to grow up in the Lord. That pastor won't settle for mediocrity in those he leads. His love for God and His people causes him to compel excellence from those he shepherds. If money is short, love makes him dig into his own pockets. If someone is hungry, it opens his refrigerator and cabinets. If someone is sick, it visits the hospital and prays for him or her. If someone's in jail, love pays a visit to the lockup.

When love is in the neighborhood, neighbors see about one another without an ulterior motive.

Love will stop on the side of the road to help a mom with a flat tire.

Love will prepare a meal for a senior citizen.

Love will donate clothing to the needy.

Love will provide for the needs of others without cost, without horn honking, and without the need for special awards or recognition.

This kind of love is a walk, not a sprint.

I think that the greatest proof of my ability to "walk in love" is when I've had to refocus and get past the hurt and love *anyway* with the help of the Holy Spirit.

Jesus asks us, "If you love those who love you, what reward will you get? Are not even the tax collectors doing that?" (Matthew 5:46). It's easy to love lovable people, the downtrodden, or the innocent. But loving someone who *exploits* you, *abandons* you, and is inconsistent in demonstrating his or her love, loyalty, or commitment to your relationship is a hard kind of love to walk in. This happens to God all the time, but because He is love, He remains constant, and He never changes. His love is unabated and relentless. His love doesn't yield no matter how we mistreat Him, no matter how ugly our sins are. And if I am to be like Him, the place He starts the metamorphosis is in my heart.

Because of this reality, my daily prayer is, "Lord, replace my heart of flesh and give me Your heart of love."

**God's Love
Is Not Indifferent.
It Is a Priceless Stone That Brings Endless Ripples.**

CHAPTER 5

Love and Patience Hang Out Together

Love is patient.

—1 Corinthians 13:4

I believe God teaches us to love by putting some unlovely people around us. It takes no character to love people who are lovely and loving to you. But unlovely people push our patience meter to the limit. They test the fiber of our character.

One day when I was in my early twenties, I decided to prepare a pot roast for dinner. I laughed as I prepared it because when I was much younger, I'd tried to fix this succulent delight, and it always came out of the oven tough and unrecognizable. Why? Because I was impatient. Much too busy to properly season the meat and give it the proper cooking time, I somehow thought I could do in an hour and a half what my mom did in three and a half or four hours. I believed that if I turned up the oven temperature to four hundred degrees, the meat would cook a lot faster and taste just as good as my mom's. Well, the step I left out was the slow boil or bake. Had I been paying proper attention; I would have noticed that she did more than season the meat and toss it in the oven. Mom seasoned the meat and left it in the refrigerator overnight so the spices could go all through it. She deftly applied her love of cooking to the roast. On Sunday morning, she put the meat into a large covered cast-iron roaster and in the oven at 250 degrees for three or four hours. By the time we got home from the church service, the whole house was filled with the delightful aroma of roast beef.

My point is this: How undone, tough, and flavorless would we be if God hadn't been lovingly patient with us? It has taken Him years of loving patience to properly season us into what He wants us to be. He has used our joys, trials, troubles, tragedies, disappointments, misfortunes, and many other life situations to *season* us for His use. Imagine what you and I would look like if God had just turned up the heat full tilt on us. What if He acted like us when we behaved badly? Suppose God just zapped us when we were disobedient. Thank God He doesn't. Instead, "He is patient with you, not wanting anyone to perish, but everyone to come to repentance" (2 Peter 3:9). Like the loving parent He is, God is patient, wanting us to get it right and reach our full potential in Him.

It occurs to me how patient God has been with me, and I am positive that He expects me to be just as patient with others. He doesn't want me to become an amnesiac about how deeply forgiving and patient He has been with me. Sometimes when I encounter individuals whose lives have been wrecked by sin, it's easy to rush to judgment and condemnation on them. That's when the Holy Spirit reminds me that I dare not forget the heavy debt God canceled for me with the sacrifice of Jesus Christ at Calvary.

Review the following passages and comment on how God has been patient toward you and how your impatience has been costly for you.

Psalm 90:4

2 Peter 3:8–9

Hebrews 10:36–37

What does love look like? It has hands to help others.
It has the feet to hasten to the poor and needy. It has
eyes to see misery and want. It has the ears to hear the
sighs and sorrows of men. That is what love looks like.

—Augustine

Light on the Word

Jesus told of the unforgiving servant in Matthew 18:23–34. In short, a servant owed a king several million dollars. He was unable to repay the money and was on his way, along with his family, to a debtor's prison. He begged the king to be patient and merciful, and the king relented, canceled the debt, and let him go (v. 26).

It would be nice if the story ended there, but unfortunately, amnesia set in, and the forgiven man sought out someone who owed him. Check this out: "But when that servant went out he found one of his fellow servants who owed him a hundred denarii [a few dollars]. He grabbed him and began to choke him. Pay back what you owe me! He demanded. *His fellow servant fell to his knees and begged him, 'Be patient with me, and I will pay you back.' But he refused. Instead, he went off and had the man thrown into prison until he could repay the debt"* (Matthew 18:26–30, emphasis added).

Patience leads to understanding. Perhaps this story will help to illustrate more clearly what I mean:

Back in the mid–1980s, when I was a struggling single mom with a whole lot of debt and not much income, I owed a certain bank. The monthly payments were too high, and try as I might, no one would listen to me when I tried to get them lowered. So, I paid the bank what I was able to every month. They insisted that I pay what they wanted regardless of my situation and decided to sue me in civil court for the entire balance of over $800. Though I was working at that time, I was earning only around nine dollars an hour. There was no extra anything. I remember going to court very much afraid, unable to afford legal counsel, and armed only with my faith, an envelope of payment receipts, and my monthly budget.

The magistrate listened to the bank's attorney and then gave me a chance to explain why I hadn't been making the total payment each month. I just told the truth: that I had been raising my two children without financial help, that my income was the only money I had. I provided him with all my bills, payment receipts, and my monthly household expense sheet.

He took all the information into his office and asked all parties to wait until he had reviewed the documents. During that half hour, I quietly sat in the courtroom and prayed. I caught a glimpse of the smug look on the bank representative's face when the magistrate returned to his bench. The magistrate cleared his throat and said, "I have reviewed all documents provided by both parties, and while I understand the bank wants all their money every month, I also have a realistic picture of what's going on with Mrs. Massey."

He said, "Gentlemen, she has been paying you something every month on time. I see, based on her phone records, that she has called your corporate office several times, attempting to get the payment lowered, and you refused. Also, you have continued to tack on late payments and interest. You also expect her to pay court costs and attorney fees. Gentlemen, this is a single parent with two young children, who has not reneged on a debt. Your demands will cause undue hardship, and I cannot allow you to do this. I find in favor of Mrs. Massey in this matter. She does not owe any late fees since she has not been late. Her payments are now lowered to the amount she's been paying you every month. She is not required to pay your court costs and attorney fees. That's my ruling, gentlemen. Case dismissed!"

If not for impatience, the case would never have gone to court. Had the bank bothered to get an understanding, the issue could have been resolved long before judicial intervention. The judge said, "Case dismissed."

To us the Lord says, "Forgiven, debt canceled, justified!"

Love and patience hang out together.

Review the scriptures related to love below and write your thoughts for each one.

Exodus 20:6

Leviticus 19:18

Psalm 63:3

Psalm 130:7

Proverbs 3:11–12

Proverbs 17:17

Matthew 22:37–39

1 John 3:1

Reflections and Prayer

Genuine love is more than just a feeling. It calls forth action. Sometimes unconditional love is inconvenient and tedious.

Consider the price Jesus paid for love. He gave His very life! Going to Calvary wasn't convenient. It's much easier to talk about love than to demonstrate it.

Dear Lord, teach us how to love in deed and not only in word. Help us to put others before ourselves without grumbling, complaining, and judging. Teach us the purity and joy of real love. In the name of Jesus, we pray. Amen.

Love
Love deep, unfathomable, inexplicable. Love
gracious, Sweet, profound, and real.
Love unconditional, without limit, unbound, untethered.
Love pure and holy.
Love, God's most precious gift to man expressed in
Jesus Christ.

—LeVerta Massey

BOOK 2

Stripped, Beaten, and Half Dead: Compassion Is a Priceless Stone

CHAPTER 6

Go and Do Likewise

An expert in the law wanting to justify himself asked Jesus, "Who is my neighbor?"

In reply, Jesus said: "A man was going down from Jerusalem to Jericho when he fell into the hands of robbers. They stripped him of his clothes, beat him and went away, leaving him half dead. A priest happened to be going down the same road, and when he saw the man, he passed by on the other side. So too, a Levite, when he came to the place and saw him, passed by on the other side. But a Samaritan, as he traveled, came where the man was; and when he saw him, he took pity [had compassion] on him. He went to him and bandaged his wounds, pouring on oil and wine. Then he put the man on his donkey, took him to an inn and took care of him. The next day he took out two silver coins and gave them to the innkeeper. 'Look after him,' he said, 'and when I return, I will reimburse you for any extra expense you may have.'

Which of these three do you think was a neighbor to the man who fell into the hands of robbers?"

The expert in the law replied, "The one who had mercy [compassion] on him."

Jesus told him, "Go and do likewise." (Luke 10:30–37, emphasis added)

Note that the unidentified man was "going down" from Jerusalem to Jericho. Jerusalem was the center of Jewish worship. Many of the people we deal with every day are not much different from this man, who was accosted by robbers. Perhaps they haven't been physically abused as he was, but spiritually, they're no better off. They go up to worship the Lord, joined by their brothers and sisters, but before, during, or afterward they leave the sanctity of the church; they are robbed of their joy, stripped of their dignity, and left half dead by legalistic, unthinking fellow Christians.

Many years ago, I was a member of a church with strict rules governing the clothes you wore to services. I vividly recall being in line in the dining hall for dinner after service one Sunday when a brand-new member of the body of Christ (we'll call her Maryann) came and stood in line behind me. She was radiant with the joy of having just surrendered her life. Her mom and dad had been praying for years that she would abandon her drug and alcohol dependency and allow God to rule her life. Finally, she had taken the first of many steps. Life had left her beaten, stripped, and abandoned. As we were waiting for our meal, one of the older women of the church came over to hug and congratulate her; but before she finished, she looked down and saw she wasn't wearing a skirt but a pair of "gauchos." She said, "I'm glad you came to the Lord today, but you can't wear those pants in here. We don't wear pants." (Before you ask, no, she didn't offer to share clothes with her.)

I stood there and saw the joy draining from Maryann. She was a babe in Christ, who had been living in the streets for years. She didn't have a closet full of expensive clothes and shoes; nor could she afford them. She had gone up to Jerusalem to worship and surrender her life to God and went down robbed of her joy, stripped of her dignity, and left half dead by a "sister in the Lord."

Some of us who witnessed this travesty tried to encourage Maryann to ignore the exchange with the older woman and to come to church in whatever she had; we said that God looks on the heart, not the outward appearance. We even offered to take her shopping and raid our closets to provide her with more clothing. She was deeply wounded. She never returned to that church. I truly hope she remained somewhere in the body of Christ.

Respond to the following questions:

1. Have you ever been wounded in the body of Christ?
2. How did you feel?
3. Did you take your hurts to the Lord? If not, why?
4. Did you experience God's compassion through His people? If not, what happened?

It's not too late to talk to Jesus about your hurts. He will gladly exchange your pain for joy and heal your wounded heart.

CHAPTER 7

Who Is My Neighbor? (Personal Evangelism Will Cost You Something)

This passage of scripture (Luke 10:30–37) is more than just a story of a nice guy who pitied someone who was down on his luck. It's more than a story of a Samaritan who did the right thing. It's an illustration of personal evangelism at its highest degree. Let's examine this passage more closely:

First, the young lawyer thought his neighbor was only someone he lived next to in a nice, comfortable neighborhood. He was probably more concerned with being close friends and neighbors with those who fit his socio-economic profile. Today he would probably give to several charities to soothe his conscience and feel good about that. He could quote some scriptures and was well versed in the Mosaic Law. Words like *compassion* and *mercy* probably made him uncomfortable. How many of us are willing to throw some money or unsolicited advice at a problem, hoping it will just go away? How often are we critical of those who need mercy or forgiveness—that is, until it's our turn to need the same? Walk a mile in your sister or brother's shoes.

Second, Jesus was able to discern the man's motives and answered his question in such a way that his self-exalting pride crumbled right before his eyes. He let him know that stripped, beaten, and half-dead people were his neighbors, and pretending not to see them was not (and is not) acceptable to God.

The third blow to the lawyer's ego was that a Samaritan (a half-breed) had gone out of his way to aid the victim. Historically, the area between Jerusalem and Jericho was known at that time to be a treacherous place to travel by day or night. I'm sure the young lawyer wouldn't have dreamed of stopping to help the man.

Light on the Word

We never read in scripture where the Samaritan spoke a word to the wounded man; nor did he express concern for his own safety. He didn't whine about how much of his time he had spent on the man. Instead, he did the following:

⇨ He went to the wounded man.
⇨ He bandaged up his wounds.
⇨ He put the man on his donkey (probably walked the rest of the way).
⇨ He made sure someone took care of the stranger (neighbor).
⇨ He paid the expenses for the man (Luke 10:33–34).

He demonstrated *real* faith and compassion. Personal evangelism will cost you something. Expect to be inconvenienced. Are you willing to pay the price? Are you willing to cast this stone? This priceless stone is compassion.

Quietly reflect on the following questions.

1. Have you ever been in a situation where you needed help but didn't receive it? How did that make you feel?
2. Have you ever intentionally avoided someone you knew was in trouble? How did you justify your actions?
3. Is there ever a good reason for refusing someone in need? When unsure what to do, consider asking God for direction.

CHAPTER 8

Demonstrate Compassion to the World

Compassion won't allow us to turn our heads away from the individual Satan has ambushed and left for dead. When people in the world see real compassion in the people of God, they get a close-up view of the character of Jesus Christ. They can see He is not only our Savior but indeed has become our Lord.

How many times have you heard someone say, "If he or she is a Christian, I don't want to be one"? I have overheard this many times in my life, usually after one of my Christian brothers or sisters has just reacted poorly to one of life's many unplanned events.

I can recall that one day Tammi (not real name), who had moved into my former apartment, was trying to relight the pilot on the furnace and must have allowed the gas to escape too long. When she bent over to guide a piece of lighted newspaper into the pilot area of the furnace, the fire whooshed out at her face and singed her eyebrows, lashes, and both her cheeks. She panicked! Her face must have felt like it was on fire. She ran out of the basement and into the cold Michigan winter air, dashing to the next-door neighbor's house. She couldn't afford a phone since she was raising three little children alone.

Frantically, Tammi banged on the door and rang the bell. Finally, the neighbor came to the door and asked what she wanted. Tammi explained what had happened as calmly as she could while standing on the cold porch in her house slippers and robe. When she finished, the devout *Christian* woman looked at her and said, "I have a meeting to go to this morning, and I don't have time to take you to the emergency room." Then she abruptly closed her door.

A few minutes later, Tammi knocked on my door. I had moved to a small house only two doors down from her. I opened the door, and the first things I saw were her singed hair, eyebrows, and the pink skin on her cheeks and forehead. Her little girl was with her and crying, saying over and over, "My mommy got burned. My mommy got burned!"

I looked at her more closely and noticed that her right hand had been badly burned, not just singed.

On the way to the emergency room, I asked her what had happened, and she told me about trying to relight the furnace because it had gone out during the night. After having lived there for many years, I knew all too well about that old furnace.

The doctor said she had second-degree burns on her right hand and only minor burns on her face. He gave her some burn ointment, loosely bandaged her hand, wrote her a prescription for pain, and sent her home, all in about forty minutes. On the way home, I invited her and the children to church and dinner on Sunday, and she accepted. Before I let her out in front of her apartment, she asked me what church I belonged to, and when I told her, she looked at me and said, "The lady next door invited me to that church! When I asked her for help this morning, she said she had a meeting to go to and closed the door in my face." The words tumbled out of her mouth followed by bitter tears.

"She's always telling me that I need to be saved and that being a Christian will change my life. If she calls herself a *Christian*, then

I don't want to be one!" Then she got out of my car, pulled her daughter out, and slammed the door.

I sat there in front of the apartment, stunned, feeling as though someone had just slapped my face. I wrestled with Tammi's last words all night long. *If she calls herself a Christian, then I don't want to be one.* I prayed for her and her children throughout the evening and into the early morning hours. I prayed because I knew how much a young single mother needed Jesus. I knew it because I had been a single mom and had been able to raise my two youngest children only due to God's help.

Tammi didn't come to church that Sunday, but I made it my mission not to let a day go by without checking on her and the children. The Holy Spirit told me to be quiet about asking her to come to church and to concentrate on being kind and loving toward her. He kept bringing the scripture back to me. "I have loved you with an everlasting love; I have drawn you with loving-kindness" (Jeremiah 31:3). It is God's love for us, not our love for Him, that is the basis for our salvation. His love is expressed through our compassion for others. Tammi and I became close friends after a while, and her guard came down concerning the things of God. I was blessed to effectively witness to Tammi by showing her real compassion, not merely rendering lip service. One Sunday I looked up, and there she was. She came and gave her life to the Lord. *Only the angels in heaven could have rejoiced more than I have!*

Shortly after her surrender, she was brutally murdered and left in a field to die. I know she's home with the Lord. Before her death, I watched God transform her whole life. She rarely smiled before being saved. She never talked about her dreams of becoming a licensed childcare provider and eventually opening a daycare center. It was as though the Lord opened a new world before her. The light of Christ was turned on for the first time in her life, and she glowed in her rebirth.

God has given us choices in life. One of those is to allow Him to *demonstrate His love* through us by acts of *compassion*.

Try casting this priceless stone into someone's life today and watch God perform a miracle before your very eyes.

Consider the following questions and respond:

1. How were you drawn to God by His loving-kindness?
2. How did you feel when you first experienced God's compassion and mercy?
3. When did you last show compassion and mercy toward another person? What were the results?

Review the scriptures related to compassion below and write your thoughts for each:

Nehemiah 9:17

Isaiah 54:10

Zechariah 7:9–10

Matthew 14:13–14

Romans 9:15–16

Colossians 3:12

James 5:11

Reflections and Prayer

Compassion is defined as sorrow for another's sufferings; pity.

In Colossians 3:12, Paul admonished us "as God's chosen people, holy and dearly loved, [to] clothe yourselves with compassion."

In other words, beloved, be covered, wrapped up, and immersed in compassion. Let it so become part of who you are that you can give it liberally, without hesitation, from your heart.

Kind and compassionate Father, thank You for the loving-kindness and compassion You have shown us through Your Son, Jesus Christ. Bless us, Lord, to show we are yours by the way we show Your love and compassion to others. Amen.

Compassion Is a Priceless
Stone
That Brings Endless Ripples

I have found in life that no matter how low I've been or what my moods or inclinations have been, when I've been selfish and my heart has overflowed with unforgiveness and anger, Jesus has compassion for me. He didn't condemn me but spoke comforting words to me. In my rebellion, He was that true friend who spoke the truth to me in love. He became the "friend that sticketh closer than a brother."

Cast the priceless stone of compassion and watch God change lives around you. The ripples caused by compassion will last a lifetime.

BOOK 3

Faith in God Is A Priceless Stone

CHAPTER 9

Faith in God Impacts Lives

Now when Daniel learned that the decree had been
published, he went home to his upstairs room where
the windows opened toward Jerusalem. Three times
a day he got down on his knees and prayed, giving
thanks to his God, just as he had done before.

—Daniel 6:10

The remarkable thing to me about Holy Scripture is that each time
I look at a passage, I see something different—another glimpse into
the awesome mind of God. I've probably read about Daniel twenty
times, and each time I am awed by how his faith in God and his
faithfulness to God impacted the lives of an entire kingdom of people,
including their supreme ruler, the king.

I had a friend who lived to be ninety-one years old. What stands
out most in my mind about "Big Ma," as she was affectionately called,
was her faith in God. She believed God would provide for her, no
matter what. Her faith spurred her faithfulness to God through the
years. Even when she became too ill to attend church every Sunday,
she sent her offering and even tithed on her meager pension. I was
a young woman who was struggling to raise two little children and
go to college without much money and not a whole lot of wisdom.

She took me under her wings, nurtured me, and shared her years of God-given wisdom. She often said to me, "Take care of God's business, and God will take care of yours." When I became weary in doing well, she sensed the heaviness I felt and said, "God sees, baby. Stay faithful till death." It seems I can still hear her saying those words over a cup of too- strong coffee. I remember seeing her reach down in her bosom to pull out a knotted handkerchief that contained her offering for Sunday service. She never wavered in her faith or her faithfulness to God. She never failed to encourage others, even in her sickness.

As I reread Daniel 6, my mind ventured back to those times with my friend, and I began to evaluate my faithfulness to a faithful God. How would I react if I were in Daniel's shoes? In my friend's shoes? Perhaps my lions' den won't be literal, but maybe it will be sickness, poverty, or persecution. What will my testimony be to the world? What will your testimony be?

Review the scriptures related to faithfulness below and write your thoughts for each one.

2 Kings 20:5–6

Psalm 85:10–11

Psalm 100:5

Matthew 12:21

John 14:12

Romans 1:17

1 Timothy 6:12

Hebrews 11:6

CHAPTER 10

Faith When Things Get Tight

Daniel's life of faith and faithfulness caused his enemies and King Darius to notice he served God *continually*. They took note of the fact that this wasn't like some relationship with a human-made god. His enemies had taken note that even though an edict was issued against worshipping anyone but the king, he still prayed to his God three times a day without fail. They conspired to use his faith in his God against him. Rain or shine, he sought God. The godly and the godless took note. His faith in a faithful God caused him to have this testimony when the king came to the lions' den after a sleepless night. The king called to Daniel and said, "Daniel, servant of the living God, has your God, whom you serve continually, been able to rescue you from the lions?" (Daniel 6:20). In other words, "How's that faith thing working for you, Daniel?"

Daniel answered, "O king, live forever! My God sent his angel, and he shut the mouths of the lions. They have not hurt me, because I was found innocent in his sight. Nor have I ever done any wrong before you, O king" (Daniel 6:20–22).

When we live a life of faith in God, we too can have a testimony that will cause men to trust our God and bring us favor. Daniel's unwavering faith demonstrated the power and might of our God better than any acts of piety ever would. The priceless stone of faith was cast into the lives of the people when Daniel remained faithful to his God, regardless of the circumstances.

The ripples are still going on centuries after he has left the scene. When all was said and done, the king gave this testimony about Daniel's God: "I issue a decree that in every part of my kingdom people must fear and reverence the God of Daniel. For he is the living God and he endures forever; His kingdom will not be destroyed; his dominion will never end. He rescues, and he saves; he performs signs and wonders in the heavens and on the earth. He has rescued Daniel from the power of the lions" (Daniel 6:26–27.

Review Hebrews 11:1 and prayerfully consider the following questions:

1. Does anyone believe your God is real because of your faith in Him?
2. Is God using you to make an impact on someone's life (family, friends, coworkers)?
3. Will your faith in God withstand ridicule from unbelievers?

CHAPTER 11

He Who Promised Is Faithful

Let us hold fast the confession of our hope without wavering, for He who promised is faithful.

—Hebrews 10:23

This scripture reminds me of someone I met many years ago. Mary (not her real name) was married to an unsaved man. She told me he was mean to her every day but especially as Sunday approached. The enemy used him to test her faith in God. Undaunted, she got up early every Sunday morning and prepared his meals, since he wouldn't eat food prepared the night before. She ironed his clothes and cleaned the house thoroughly so he wouldn't have any excuse for mistreating her. Still, he found fault and tried to pick fights with her on Sunday mornings. The more abusive he became, the more Mary resolved to remain faithful to her God, and the more she cried out to God on her husband's behalf. She believed God would save him no matter how things looked.

We Walk by Faith and Not by Sight

One Sunday morning, after the couple had been married for over forty years, she was preparing to walk out the door on her way to church when she glanced over her shoulder, and behind her stood her husband. He was dressed in a new suit and had his hat in his hand. She turned to him and asked, "Where are you going?"

"I'm going to church with you!" he replied. For probably only the tenth time since they were married, he was going to church. Previously, he had attended church only for funerals and his four children's weddings.

Mary later asked him what had made him decide to come to church. He told her it was her faithfulness that had convinced him to give his life to the Lord. That day he repented for his meanness and ingratitude for what God had given him. He recalled that she had done everything she could to make him happy and that even through his tirades she remained sweet and never stopped being faithful to God.

She shared her testimony with me one Saturday afternoon in the parking lot of our favorite grocery store. It blesses me to think that when we remain faithful to God, He is faithful to us. It encouraged me to continue to pray for individuals I felt would never receive Christ as their Savior.

Mary's story happened many years ago, and since then, not only did her husband accept Christ but also did many of his friends from work and unsaved family members too. And the ripples from that priceless stone of faith keep going on and going.

Review Hebrews 11:6 and Romans 8:24. Prayerfully consider the following questions:

1. Think about your family and friends. Is there anyone you have given up on receiving Christ?
2. Are you willing to seek God more diligently on his or her behalf?

Light on the Word

If we are faithless, *He* will remain faithful,
for He cannot disown himself.
—2 Timothy 2:13 (emphasis added)

God loves us so much that even when our faith is shaky, He remains faithful. He already knew life would test our faith to its limits. Faith isn't proved genuine until it's tested.

Several decades ago, a dear friend was struggling with sickle cell anemia and kidney disease. We were regular prayer partners, and she often expressed that she didn't understand how God could allow her to have so much pain. Her greatest desire was to have children and watch them grow up and have families of their own.

Even though she rarely had a day without excruciating pain in her joints, she still believed God would bless her with children and grandchildren. The doctors told her she shouldn't have children because the odds were great that they also would suffer from sickle cell disease. Despite her doctor's prediction, she had a beautiful daughter in 1976 and then a son in 1978.

She told me that God had promised her she would have healthy children and that her grandchildren wouldn't be stricken with the disease.

Fast-forward to 2013, and although she passed away in 2009 from complications of sickle cell, her children and six grandchildren are all healthy. Praise be to God! Even though she suffered greatly, her faith in the one who promised remained steadfast.

So whenever I find myself teetering toward self-pity, I consider my childhood friend. I think about her unwavering faith in and faithfulness to a God who can do the impossible.

Prayerfully consider the following questions and respond:

1. Read 2 Peter 3:9. What has God promised you that you're still waiting for?
2. Read Luke 1:37. What does this scripture mean to you?

> If you do not stand firm in your faith,
> You will not stand at all.
>
> —Isaiah 7:9

What does it mean to stand firm in our faith? When we are resolute in our faith, this quiets and composes our minds. Sometimes our lives might seem like we're standing on the deck of a rickety ship during a violent nor'easter. At some point, we must grab hold of something unshakeable to steady us, and that is our faith in God. The writer of Hebrews 10:23 said, "Let us hold unswervingly [hold fast] to the hope we profess, for he who promised is faithful."

Stay faithful to Jesus during life's stormy days. God is always faithful. Will you remain faithful (hold fast) to Him in the storm? Here's how I remain faithful in the storm:

> ➤ I don't pretend everything's all right with me when it's not. I tell God how I feel. With God you can't "fake it, until you make it." He knows you. Be transparent. Be honest with Him.
>
> ➤ I find scripture about God's promises to me and meditate on them. Sometimes I sing psalms to Him like "Thy loving-kindness is better than life!"
>
> ➤ I love to spend time with God early in the morning, like 5:30 a.m. Read Psalm 5:3 for encouragement.

Faith Is a Priceless Stone
That Brings Endless Ripples

Reflections and Prayer

In the face of what seemed to be insurmountable suffering and hardship, the apostle Paul uttered three words that have encouraged my heart over the years: "I believe God" (Acts 27:25). Believing God means taking Him at His word. Over the years I've heard people referred to as having great faith. I'd rather have faith in a great God.

He is completely reliable. God is faithful even when I am faithless, when I can't see my way through. When everything around me falls apart, God doesn't. We live at a time when many profess faith *in* God but don't believe God. There is a vast difference.

> Lord, I thank You that even amid trying situations,
> You are there. I will remain faithful, even though I
> don't always fully understand everything. You are still
> in control and faithful to those who are Yours.
> We can, therefore, praise You in our trials.
> Hallelujah and amen!

Hang Out with Victorious People

In the society we live in, it's not hard to become discouraged or weary in doing well. I have learned that if we're not vigilant, the stuff of life can cause our faith in God to fizzle out completely. That's why it's so vital that we stay in the word, why we must spend time with our brothers and sisters in the Lord and pray continually. Hebrews 10:25 admonishes us, "Let us not give up meeting together, as some are in the habit of doing, but let us encourage one another—and all the more as you see the Day approaching."

Our adversary, the devil, loves to keep us from hearing the victorious testimonies of fellow believers. He knows our faith is energized when we hear what God has done for others. So, he lies to us and says things like, "You don't need to go to church to be a Christian" or "Go next week. The game is on today" or "They don't like you anyway. Why go?" If you decide to acquiesce to his nonsense and stay home, the very thing you needed to hear will be missed.

Just imagine for a moment that Joseph had decided to abandon his faith in God. An entire nation would have been impacted. If anyone had a reason to give up, it was him. Genesis 37–47 chronicles his life and tells us that his brothers were jealous of him and sought to get rid of him because he was his father's (Jacob's) favorite son. His brothers betrayed him, put him in a pit, then sold him into slavery. He was imprisoned and wrongly accused, but he finally ended up as second in command in Egypt. You never read that he spent time grumbling about his circumstances. Instead, because of his faith, God used him mightily to the saving of a nation amid a great famine. Even when Joseph could've taken credit for his ability to interpret Pharaoh's dream, he remained faithful to God and said, "I cannot do it, but God will give Pharaoh the answer he desires" (Genesis 41:16).

God greatly rewarded his faith. I spoke earlier of how the godly and ungodly will testify of our faith in God. Scripture bears this out in Genesis 41:38–44. A pagan pharaoh repeatedly said, "Can we find anyone like this man, one in whom is the spirit of God?" (41:37). "Since God has made all this known to you, there is no one so discerning and wise as you." (41:39); and "I hereby put you in charge of the whole land of Egypt." (41:41) Can you say "favor"?

All this took place when Joseph was thirty years old. Who says faith in God doesn't have great rewards? The point here is that our faith and trust in God don't go unnoticed.

Luke 18:29–30 speaks of the rewards believers receive for their faith in Christ. Jesus said, "I tell you the truth, no one who has left home or wife or brothers or parents or children for the sake of the kingdom of God will fail to receive many times as much in this age and, in the age to come, eternal life." Faith in Christ has many benefits and sacrifices. Sometimes familial relationships suffer because of our faith. Even lifelong friendships might sag, or a great job might be lost. Whatever the sacrifice, Christ more than makes up for our sacrifices with His great love for us and miraculous provision. The psalmist wrote, "Though my father and mother forsake me, the Lord will receive me" (Psalm 27:10).

What do the following scriptures tell us about God's faithfulness to the faithful?

2 Samuel 22:26

Psalm 31:23

Psalm 100:5

Psalm 145:13

Matthew 25:21

Romans 3:3–4

1 John 1:9

2 Thessalonians 3:3

Light on the Word

Faith *(for the purposes of this writing)* is defined as, "trust in the person of Jesus, the truth of His teaching, and the redemptive work He accomplished at Calvary".

Sometimes our faith gets shaky or evaporates completely. Romans 3:3 says, "What if some did not have faith? Will their lack of faith nullify God's faithfulness?" Paul's response to this question is in verse 4; he said, "Not at all! Let God be true, and every man a liar."

If all the world's greatest educators formed a coalition to disprove God's faithfulness, all their high-minded defenses couldn't stand against God's firmly fixed truth. The chronic unfaithfulness of people doesn't alter the fact that God's faithfulness doesn't change (Psalm 116:11). The self-seeking, truth-suppressing cannot change God's faithfulness. God's plan for His people won't change because men chose to reject the truth and follow evil (Romans 2:8). The truth of God remains the truth, no matter who doesn't believe it. Let every man be a liar!

"Can we find a friend so faithful; who will all our sorrows share?"

Paul encouraged Timothy by writing, "Here is a trustworthy saying: If we died with him, we will also live with him; if we endure, we will also reign with him. If we disown him, he will also disown us; if we are faithless, he will remain faithful, for he cannot disown himself" (2 Timothy 2:11–13). God's faithfulness far outstrips our obedience. In fact, it is pointless to try to make God's faithfulness in any way dependent on the standard of our faith or obedience because our righteousness will never measure up to God's. Isaiah 64:6 says, "All of us have become like one who is unclean, and all our righteous acts are like filthy rags; we all shrivel up like a leaf, and like the wind, our sins sweep us away." This doesn't mean we shouldn't attempt to live a faithful life before God, only that His acceptance of us isn't based on our "good" behavior. He doesn't keep a "performance meter" for each of us.

The stone called *faith*, when exercised, has the potential to change the lives of our families, friends, coworkers, neighborhood, and the world. Cast this stone every day, and God will bless you greatly.

BOOK 4

The Peace of God:
A Priceless Stone

CHAPTER 12

Peace That Transcends Human Understanding

And the *peace* of God, which transcends
all understanding, will guard your hearts
and minds in Christ Jesus.
—Philippians 4:7 (emphasis added)

Sarah and Jim Pearson (not real names) got married on March 18, 1978, and for thirty years enjoyed the slower pace of Midwest living. They had grown together in their love for one another and their love for God. Sarah told about how their marriage had been normal as marriages go. She and Jim had the usual growing pains of learning to live together after coming from their parents' homes. They had to learn to manage their finances and buy wisely. When their four daughters came along, Sarah and Jim saved and planned with great joy. They decided early on that each girl would have a college education first and then marry a Christian man.

Janice, Cheryl, Olivia, and Marsha grew up to be beautiful and godly young women. They all graduated from college except Olivia. She decided that four years of studying just weren't for her.

Instead, she opted for and completed paralegal training and shortly after that began working at a law firm. Olivia enjoyed her work, but she was restless and longed to be someplace exciting like Florida or California. Her parents were hesitant about encouraging her to venture away from home and family; however, they didn't openly criticize or discourage her. Rather, Sarah and Jim prayed and asked God to give them peace and to direct Olivia's steps.

Olivia decided to leave Michigan in October 1999 and headed for Berkley, California. She had applied for several paralegal positions and after three interviews (in California) had finally been called by one of the best firms in San Francisco, just a short trip across the Bay. She loved her job and quickly became caught up in the hustle and bustle of Bay Area living. San Francisco is alive twenty-four hours a day, seven days a week.

Her parents became deeply concerned for her spiritual well-being and her safety. Her letters became scarce, and when she did write, she no longer mentioned God and didn't say whether she had found a church home.

Jim and Sarah asked their church family to keep Olivia on the prayer list. They began to fast two days a week for their daughter, every Wednesday and Friday without fail. Sarah fasted until dinner; Jim fasted until lunch, since he did hard physical work. God gave them the peace they needed to sustain them through those trying times.

Read Matthew 17:10–21 and respond to the following questions:

1. Can you recall situations in your life where peace was the direct result of fasting and prayer? Did you share your testimony?

After a few weeks, the members of the congregation noticed a radical change in Jim and Sarah's worship. It became more intense and affected the way people around them worshipped. Jim no longer stood stoically, clapping when prompted by the praise and worship leaders. He lifted his hands high unto God, and Sarah likewise no longer just went through the motions but immersed herself as though drenched by God's presence. Although neither of them knew what was going on with Olivia, there was a peace surrounding them that boggled the minds of everyone who knew them.

"And let the peace [soul harmony, which comes] from Christ rule [act as umpire continually] in your hearts [deciding and settling with finality all questions that arise in your minds, in that peaceful state] to which as [members of Christ's] one body you were also called [to live]. And be thankful [appreciative], [giving praise to God always]" (Colossians 3:15 AMP).

In the game of baseball, the umpire is behind home plate, where he has a broad view of the entire game. The umpire settles all scoring disputes, and his decisions are final.

Our hearts are the seat of our emotions, just like home plate. And like the umpire, the peace of God settles every dispute whether spiritual or natural.

Light on the Word

Imagine never being worried about anything. Is that even possible? Is it possible to have peace when there's chaos all around us? We turn on the news, and all we see are unrest and mayhem everywhere; pick up a newspaper—peace treaties made and then broken, more unrest, and more chaos. On the job we see still more. When we drive down the road, people are zipping around recklessly and suffering from *road rage*. Sometimes there's even chaos in the body of Christ. Yes, in the church! Road rage.

The word of God says, "The peace of God, which transcends all understanding, will guard your hearts and your minds in Christ Jesus" (Philippians 4:7).

The peace of God isn't like the world's peace. It doesn't come from self-help books or warm, fuzzy feelings. It comes from knowing

God is absolutely in control, even when things appear to be spiraling into the abyss.

Read John 16:33 and Colossians 3:15, prayerfully consider the following questions, and respond.

1. Can you recall an incident when you had to seek the peace of God in your life? What were the results?
2. How did God let you know He was there to reassure and comfort you?

Reflections and Prayer

Consider ways in which you have relinquished your peace and allowed circumstances to dictate your reactions. At those times, did you pray and fast? Did you invite almighty God into the situation? Or did you seek the world's opinion?

Lord, in times of unrest, we invite You to come in and
calm the raging seas. Teach us to rely on You for peace.
Amen.

CHAPTER 13

Peaceful and Steadfast in God

After two years, letters from their precious Olivia stopped coming altogether. Sarah wrote, but the letters came back unopened and stamped "Addressee unknown." Instead of having panic, however, they had "the peace that transcends all understanding." Their friends, Jim's coworkers, their fellow church members, and family members were all scratching their heads in disbelief. *How could they be so calm? How come they still had peace? Weren't they concerned about their daughter? After all, San Francisco was a big place, and all kinds of horrible things could happen there.* They even urged Jim to get on a plane and find Olivia, even offered to pay his fare. But still they remained peaceful and steadfast in their devotion to God, in their belief that God had everything under His control.

During this period of their lives, Jim and Sarah clung to Jesus's words in John 14:27. "Peace I leave with you, my peace I give you. I do not give to you as the world gives. Do not let your hearts be troubled and do not be afraid."

One evening during dinner, the phone shrilled, jolting them from the usual family dinnertime banter. Jim answered, still chewing, and through the static he heard his beloved Olivia's voice for the first time in nearly three years. It was June 4, 1999. She said, "Daddy! Are you there?"

By this time Jim was nearly choking on his food and had handed the phone to Sarah, who was right next to him when she saw the look on his face. His eyes had filled with tears, and he was struggling to swallow what was still in his mouth. When he finally composed himself, all he could say was, "Thank You, Lord! Thank You, Lord!" Once Sarah realized who was on the other end of the line, she joined her husband in rejoicing. The entire family began to rejoice and thank God for His goodness. Olivia was trying to tell them she needed to be picked up from the airport, but she had to wait until everyone had calmed down.

"Mom! Mom!" she said and waited for a response.

At last, Sarah picked up the phone and said through tears, "Olivia? Is that you? Where are you?"

Olivia answered and said, "Mom, I'm in Michigan at Metro Airport. Will someone please come and get me?"

Sarah said, "Oh yes, yes! We'll be right there. Uh, what terminal, what airline?"

Olivia gave Sarah directions and said, "Drive the van because I have a lot of stuff."

Sarah said, "Okay, we will be right there in about forty minutes."

When Sarah hung up from talking to Olivia, everyone began talking at once. "Where is she?"

"How did she get here?"

There was much excitement in the house as they prepared to pick up their daughter and sister. She was home, and it didn't matter anymore why she had stopped writing or what had happened. God had given them peace in the situation, and that peace had caused others to trust God more and believe He was working things out in their lives as well. Instead of cowering under the weight of despair and uncertainty, Jim and Sarah had rallied with praise and worship to their God.

The family chose not to give in to worry and listen to Satan's what-ifs. They chose to fast, pray, and seek God for their daughter. In exchange for utter despair, God gave them peace that transcended the understanding of everyone around them. It was a peace that caused others to desire the peace of God in their lives.

Lord, help us live in such a way
That people ask and want to know
How they can have real joy and peace
While living in a world of woe.

—Sper

1. Using scripture, explain the differences between the peace of God, peace in God, and peace with God.
2. How is true peace available to us? Read 1 Corinthians 1:3.
3. How can peace affect our decision-making? Read Colossians 3:15.
4. During times of unrest, how do we keep our hearts from becoming troubled or afraid?

CHAPTER 14

Peace and Trust Bring Great Joy

At two o'clock in the morning, everyone was still up and talking about Olivia's wonderful return home. Finally, Marsha, the youngest girl, asked the question on everyone's mind. "Olivia, where have you been the last three years, and why didn't you call Mom and Dad?"

At that everyone focused on Olivia, expecting an answer. Instead, tears began to course down her cheeks and onto the dining room table. She tried to speak, but the words stuck in her throat. Sarah reached over and gently rubbed the back of her daughter's neck, calming her. Jim silently began to pray.

When Olivia had finally calmed down, she stood up and began to speak. "Marsha, you're right. I *do* owe everybody an explanation. I'm not sure how to explain what happened to me, so I guess it's best to blurt it out. I only ask that you don't judge me too harshly. I am deeply ashamed and embarrassed about the things I've done."

Sarah's eyes filled with tears, causing the entire family to weep as well.

"You see, I got involved in a community youth group out there in San Francisco. At first, it was a lot of fun. We went on camping trips, did outreach in the poorest parts in the city, fed people at homeless shelters, and performed all kinds of great services in the surrounding communities."

"But you never mentioned any of this in your letters," Sarah said. "We didn't know what was going on."

"I know, Mom. Just let me finish, and I think you'll understand why I never said anything. You see, after a few weeks, I discovered they were a front for drug distribution.

Methamphetamines and crack cocaine were being passed out at the food pantries and homeless shelters by certain youth group members. The part that disgusted me the most was that a youth leader and his wife spearheaded the operation."

Jim asked, "Did you call the police?"

"No, Dad, I didn't because before long I was using crack cocaine and drinking too. They encouraged everyone to try it once. They said it wouldn't hurt us. The part no one told us was that it took some people only one time to become addicted. You see, for two years I was hopelessly addicted to drugs and alcohol. I had no job. I had nowhere to live. I sold most of my clothes and other belongings to get money. When I ran out of stuff to sell, I stole from stores and sold what I stole. When I got hungry, I ate what I could find in garbage cans or beg off total strangers. I begged for money on street corners."

By this time everyone was silently weeping.

"Are you clean now, Olivia?" Jim said. "I mean, do you need help? What can we do to help you, baby?"

"Daddy, praise God! I am now clean one year. It hasn't been an easy ride for me. But one day, I woke up in a homeless shelter, and all around me there was sadness. There were young women in their early twenties who looked like they were in their late fifties. The stench of old alcohol, cigarettes, and body odor was awful. There were bedbugs everywhere. I was afraid to sleep, thinking bugs would crawl into my bunk with me. One night as I sat up in the darkness, my mind cleared enough for me to realize I didn't have to live like that. I had a family who loved me. That's when I started to pray and asked God to help me get clean. You see, I wanted to come home but not before I was clean."

Sarah said, "You could have come home no matter what was going on. We would have supported you any way we could. You know that."

"Yes, Mom, I know. But you don't know how bad things were. You have no idea how low I had sunk. I couldn't put you guys through that. Anyway, as I was saying, I began to pray and ask God for help. You won't believe this, but sometimes when I was sleeping, it seemed like I could hear you and daddy praying for me. That gave me the strength and courage to move on. Early one Sunday morning, representatives from Narcotics Anonymous and Alcoholics Anonymous came through the shelter to pass out literature and answer questions. I took one of everything and decided to take part in the worship service some ministers held in the dining area."

Olivia continued, "That day an evangelist brought a word tailor made just for me. It was titled, 'You Shall Recover It All!'

"I know the Holy Spirit told her what to say. She told us to return to our father's house; that we would be received with joy. She told us the story of how the prodigal son (Luke 15:11–24) came to himself in the pigsty. When she talked about how he had made up his mind to go home and how his father had received him with open arms, it was like something inside me broke open. I couldn't stop crying. I cried for two days.

"When she finished preaching, she opened the altar and offered Christ to everyone. I acted like the woman with the issue of blood and pushed my way to the front."

Everyone in the house—Jim, Sarah, and the sisters—were clapping and praising God with gusto. Passersby probably thought a new church had opened on the block. Even the angels in heaven joined the celebration.

For the first time in over five years, that Sunday morning the whole family attended church services. Jim and Sarah beamed as they walked in with all four of their daughters.

Consider the following questions and respond:

1. Do you have family members who are addicted to drugs or alcohol?
2. Have you sought God for peace in the situation?
3. Has He given you instruction concerning the individual? Have you followed His instruction? Why or why not? Read Proverbs 16:20 prayerfully.

CHAPTER 15

Christ Has Become Our Peace

Jesus promised to leave us the Holy Spirit to remind us of all He had taught us while here on earth. Sometimes when life becomes overwhelming, we forget that God has always been here for us in the past. We tend to forget past rescues, that He has kept us in situations that seemed insurmountable. That's why journaling is an invaluable tool for the people of God. Not only will the Holy Spirit remind us of past victories, but we will have a written account of them as well.

God blesses us with *peace* not only in our personal lives but also in our interactions with fellow Christians. Because of Christ's death, we have become one, and the hostility against one another has been destroyed (Ephesians 2:14–18). Jesus has unified us through His death. He has become our peace. Now we have peace in God and with Him.

Read Luke 8:22–24 and 1 Peter 3:11, and consider the following questions:

1. Have you ever had your peace disrupted in the middle of the night?
2. Did Satan tell you things would never get any better? How did you react to the enemy's taunts?
3. Amid despair, has the Holy Spirit ever reminded you of a time when God gave you peace in a storm? How did that reassurance make you feel?

Reflection and Prayer

Consider times when fear, anger, uncertainty, doubt, anxiety, and a host of other human feelings have assaulted you. At those times the peace of God tries to move in to restrain those hostile forces and bring us comfort. But we must allow the Holy Spirit to speak peace to us; otherwise, we operate in misery and cause others to be miserable too. Pray now for the Holy Spirit to fill you with the peace of God.

> Great peace have they who love your law,
> and nothing can make them stumble.
> —Psalm 119:165

Peace, a Priceless Stone . . .

Review the scriptures related to peace below and write your thoughts for each one:

Psalm 29:11

Proverbs 14:30

Isaiah 26:3

Isaiah 32:17

Romans 5:1

1 Corinthians 7:15

1 Corinthians 14:33

Ephesians 2:14

BOOK 5

Kindness Is a Priceless Stone

CHAPTER 16

Kindness, the Noblest Weapon

Dear children, let us not love with words or
tongue but with actions and in truth.
—1 John 3:18 (NIV)

Kind: Sympathetic, friendly, gentle, benevolent.

An act of kindness isn't done out of obligation but of sweet
benevolence. True kindness is motivated by love. Kindness is a fruit
of the Spirit.

Over the years I've heard of people performing random acts of
kindness toward total strangers. Recently a friend of mine told me
that his pastor had stopped to help a homeless man on a street in St.
Louis, Missouri. He said the pastor noticed the man was wearing
broken glasses and looked very weak and weary. He invited him
into his car, took him to a McDonald's to feed him, and then called
his eye doctor to ask whether he would examine the man's eyes
and make him a new pair of glasses, which the doctor did without
cost. Because the pastor chose to minister to the man's needs first,

he didn't have a problem introducing him to Jesus Christ. The man happily accepted Jesus Christ as his Lord and Savior and has become a powerful witness for the kingdom of God and an advocate for homeless men and women.

Isn't that what Jesus did? He ministered to the physical needs of people, and then He saw to their deeper spiritual needs. Remember the five thousand men plus women and children He fed at the seashore? (Matthew 14:18–21). The disciples thought the people should have gone home to eat. Compassion moved Jesus to meet their need for food first. When they and their children were no longer hungry, Jesus could minister effectively to their spiritual needs.

Over many years of trying to reach out to individuals who don't have a personal relationship with Christ, I have learned that kindness is the noblest and most effective weapon to conquer with. "When Jesus heard what had happened [to John the Baptist], he withdrew by boat privately to a solitary place. Hearing of this, the crowds followed him on foot from the towns. When Jesus landed and saw a large crowd, he had compassion on them and healed their sick" (Matthew 14:13–14).

Before Jesus fed and ministered to the multitude, John the Baptist was beheaded. He withdrew by boat to a solitary place to grieve away from the throng of followers. Jesus showed kindness and compassion despite grieving for His cousin. Showing kindness might be inconvenient.

Companion in Pain

Jesus did some miracles as proof of His sonship. He used other miracles to teach deep truths. But in this passage we read that He healed people because He "had compassion on them." Jesus loved the people and cared deeply for them. He set aside His need to rest and to escape hostile people. When you are hurting, remember that Jesus hurts with you. He has compassion on you. Likewise, we too must be available to show compassion. We are His hands and feet.

Read Matthew 14:14–21 and consider the following questions:

1. Why do you think Jesus fed and healed people before He taught them?
2. How does kindness open the door to someone's heart?
3. What acts of kindness can you do in your neighborhood or on your job to draw others to Christ?

Light on the Word

In 1985 I was newly divorced with two young children. I was alone in Michigan with no parents, no siblings, and very few friends. I was a babe in Christ.

One day I went to the grocery store to pick up a few things. At that time money was scarce. As I checked out, I remember becoming increasingly uncomfortable as the cashier rang up my food, so I pulled a few things off the belt and was about to tell her I had changed my mind about them when I heard a man's voice behind me. "I will take care of those items for you if you don't mind."

I thought I was going to faint. When I turned around to see who was speaking, I looked up into the face of a six-foot angel with a scruffy gray beard, kind blue eyes, glasses, and a little paunch. Santa Claus—not hardly.

Once I recovered from the shock, I managed to thank him profusely. He laughed and asked me whether I had a church home and invited me to worship with him and his family.

I wondered whether he knew how much that one act of kindness encouraged me at a time when I felt so alone. It was as if God had blown me a kiss and said, "You're not alone. I'm here, and I love you."

Consider the following questions and respond:

1. Has the Holy Spirit ever prompted you to show kindness to a total stranger? Did you obey?
2. How did this make you feel inside?
3. Has someone ever unexpectedly shown you kindness? What happened?

When we are treated with kindness, it's important that we in turn show kindness. Like forgiveness, God requires us to be kind to others. James put it this way: "What good is it, my brothers, if a man claims to have faith but has no deeds? Suppose a brother or sister is without clothes and daily food. If one of you says to him, 'Go, I wish you well; keep warm and well fed,' but does *nothing* about his physical needs, what good is it?" (James 2:14–16, emphasis added).

Real faith doesn't just transform our thoughts; it also changes our behavior.

Kindness is an action word.

CHAPTER 17

Radical Thinking Required

But love your enemies, and do good, and lend expecting
nothing in return, and your reward will be great, and
you will be sons of the Most High; for He, Himself [God]
is kind [gracious] to the ungrateful and evil men.
—Luke 6:35 (HGKSB, emphasis added)

For us to show the type of love Jesus taught about, extreme radical thinking is required—a mind transfusion. He challenged their thinking in verse 32 when He asked, "If you love those who love you, what credit is that to you? Even sinners love those who love them."

The popular thinking of that day (and this one) was to show love and kindness only to those who showed it to you. But Jesus overturned the apple cart when He told them to love those who showed them no love in return. He said to give to men, expecting nothing in return; be kind to the ungrateful and the evil ones. Are you kidding? You mean, be nice to someone who intentionally harms me? Be kind to someone who can't reciprocate? How is this possible?

Without the help of the Holy Spirit, it isn't possible. Human nature says, "You be nice to me; I'll be nice to you. Be mean to me, and I'll be meaner to you." But God says, "Do not repay anyone evil for evil" (Romans 12:17). In other words, as we have become recipients of God's grace, we ought to extend that same grace to our fellow man. Consider how many times God has blessed us despite our bad behavior or foul thoughts?

I recall how this lesson was finally nailed into my brain. Several years ago, I was responsible for an employee who resented the fact that I had been promoted and not her. She went out of her way to make obnoxious remarks about me, always within earshot. Well, her birthday was approaching, and since I made a big deal of everyone else's birthday in my unit, the staff wanted to know what we were going to do for hers. My response was, "Absolutely nothing!" I justified my behavior by pointing out how hateful she had been to me.

Immediately the Holy Spirit started dealing with my spirit. He kept reminding me of Romans 12:17. "Do not repay anyone evil for evil." Of course, that was the last thing I wanted to hear. On the morning of her birthday, the Holy Spirit prevailed with me and instructed me to stop at the twenty-four-hour grocery store and get her a birthday card and specifically, a dozen tea roses. I sat in the store parking lot and wept. I wept because I wanted to be intentionally disobedient, and I felt justified in being mean to her. I'm so glad God wouldn't let me rest in my mess. I obeyed after about twenty minutes and did as the Holy Spirit had instructed. Before I left that parking lot, I repented and asked God to forgive me.

I arrived at work before anyone else in my unit, and I placed the flowers and card on her desk. When she arrived and saw the flowers and card, realizing they were from me, she came to my office and openly wept. She apologized for being so mean to me and asked my forgiveness. After that day, we never had a cross word between us. She became one of my biggest supporters. What is the point of this?

- Kindness can break down barriers between people and disarms Satan.
- Only God knows what it takes to break us down. He understands us completely.

- The lesson is rarely one sided.
- Kindness isn't always easy. Sometimes it hurts.
- Vengeance is the Lord's, not ours (Hebrews 10:30).

Light on the Word

Rachael (not real name) spoke of how she was the first African American to become a legal department supervisor at her firm in 1999. She finished law school at the top of her class and went to work for a group of attorneys. Her job required her to review cases and assign them to be adjudicated by the young attorneys and paralegals on her staff.

As life would have it, one of her staff members took exception to the fact that she was black. She said at first his actions were covert, and she naively ignored the rumblings of the rumor mill. One of her female employees came to her privately early one morning and asked to speak with her. She told Rachael that she'd overheard a fellow employee, Gerald, talking to his pod mate and telling him that he'd felt Rachael wasn't qualified to supervise anyone. He wasn't going to ask her any questions because she was probably an idiot since she was a black woman.

Rachael said her first inclination was to confront him and clear the air. She felt hurt and disappointed that someone who didn't know her had already judged her. She said the Holy Spirit ministered to her, telling her to be still—not to render evil for evil but to do good, to be kind to the young man, and to behave as though she had no idea how he felt about her. That was a lot easier said than done. Her ego was deeply bruised.

How Would You React to This Situation?

One Friday morning Rachael arrived at work early to get a jump on the day's work, and as she stepped off the elevator, she heard someone sobbing into the phone, saying, "What did I do wrong? Why are you leaving me, babe? Please, just give us a chance before you walk out!"

She tiptoed to the place the distress was coming from and peered around the cubicle wall. It was Gerald! He must have been crying for quite some time, as evident by the very large pile of tissues in the middle of his desk. Rachael avoided being seen and made her way to her office, where she quietly shut her door. Then and there she repented of her pride and began to pray for her employee. She knew about the pain of separation and divorce. Six years earlier, she had been in Gerald's shoes. Thankfully, there hadn't been children in the equation. He and his wife had two little boys to consider. She offered up a prayer for those babies as well.

Around ten o'clock that morning an urgent rap on her office door startled her. She looked up to see Gerald standing outside, waiting for access. Rachael beckoned him in and told him to have a seat. She could see the rims of his eyes were still red. "How may I help you, Gerald?" she asked.

"I need to take some time off to deal with family problems." He said this so softly that he was barely audible; his bottom lip visibly quivered.

"You want to talk about it?"

He took a deep breath to steady himself and said, "My wife has asked me for a divorce. I believe if we went to counseling, we could save our marriage. I need time to talk to her. Is it possible that I can take some time off? Please!"

His eyes overflowed with tears and stained his pale-blue shirt. He tried unsuccessfully to stem the flow with the backs of his hands.

Rachael gave him a tissue and a moment to compose himself before she responded to his request.

"Gerald, of course, you can take some time off to work on your marriage. You know we have an employee assistance program that will help you find a marriage counselor, right?" She opened her file cabinet and located a colorful brochure with all the Employee Assistance Program information he needed.

"Yes, ma'am, I know about the program. Thanks for letting me come in and talk. I wasn't sure what to do. I've never been through anything like this before. I know how busy you are, but can I just say one more thing before I go?"

"Sure, Gerald, I'm listening."

"Miss Rachael, I know you've probably heard through the grapevine that I have said some not-so-nice stuff about you and your management skills. What you heard is true. I was running my mouth, and I'm sorry."

"Gerald, why were you putting me down? Did I do or say something to offend you?"

"No, you didn't do anything to me except be kind. You could have fired me when my work wasn't up to snuff, but you didn't. You could have fired me when I got to work late every day two weeks ago, but you didn't. You knew I had been drinking last Monday and would have been justified in letting me go. Why did you let me keep my job?"

"I knew you were going through something and needed mercy, not punishment. I tried to treat you the way I would have wanted someone to treat me." Then she shared her testimony of how she had come to accept Christ.

That day Rachael and Gerald started their work relationship over again. New lines of respect were drawn, and Rachael was able to effectively witness to him about God's awesome love, mercy, grace, and kindness. He and his wife went to marriage counseling for several months and managed to salvage their foundering relationship. The best part of it all was that because of Rachael's saving faith and testimony, Gerald accepted Jesus Christ as his Lord and Savior, and then shortly thereafter, he led his wife to Jesus.

Mercy is the deepest expression of kindness.

Read the following passages of scripture related to kindness. Note your insights for each passage.

Psalm 63:3

Romans 11:22

Galatians 5:22

2 Peter 1:7

Reflections and Prayer

Kindness is an expression of God's deep love that, when passed on to other human beings, almost always alters their perception of their current circumstances. Just when they think no one cares. Just when they are down to their last dime (or meal or bus token). Just when loneliness (depression) is about to overtake their lives. Just when (you fill in the blank). God's kindness evokes heartfelt praise from those who have the good sense to appreciate it. Kindness is a priceless stone that causes endless ripples. And who knows where they stop?

Heavenly Father, thank You for every kindness You have
provided in my life. I'm not so skilled that I could earn even
one kindness. I'm so unworthy of all You freely give, yet You
give. At every opportunity, I vow to pass kindness on to others.
Your lovingkindness is indeed better than life. Therefore,
I will praise You and forever bless Your holy name!
Amen.

BOOK 6

Grace Is a Priceless Stone

CHAPTER 18

A Portrait of God's Grace

David asked, "Is there anyone still left of
the house of Saul to whom I can show
kindness [grace] for Jonathan's sake?"

—2 Samuel 9:1

Grace—Precious, Undeserved, Unexpected

Charles Spurgeon wrote, "That God would enter into gracious covenant with men is an amazing thing. That He would create man and be gracious to man is barely conceivable." For years I believed the word *grace* was what we said at every meal or what a person brought to an otherwise-classless event.

How often have we sung the old standard "Amazing Grace" without thinking about what those words mean? They are about God's unmerited favor extended to someone who doesn't deserve it and couldn't possibly earn it.

One day King David went looking for someone in his then-deceased best friend Jonathan's family, to whom He might show favor. He had previously made a vow to his dear friend that he wouldn't wipe out the family line of the previous king, as was the custom (1 Samuel 20:13–22). Remember, Jonathan was the son of David's enemy and predecessor, King Saul. Yes, that Saul—the one who tried to kill David on more than one occasion, the one who forced him to hide in caves and in the Philistine camp, and feign lunacy to preserve his life. It was also to Saul that David vowed to spare his descendants (1 Samuel 24:20–22). So David remembered his vow to Saul and Jonathan and inquired whether there was anyone left of his friend Jonathan's descendants.

What a beautiful portrait of God's grace! David didn't come up with a list of qualifiers necessary to receive his kindness. The recipient didn't have to be a certain height, weight, color, economic class, and so forth—just a descendant of Jonathan. Huddled over in the corner of a room on a pillow, in a house in Lo Debar (a dry, barren place), was a little fellow named Mephibosheth. Scripture says he was crippled in both feet because he had been dropped by his nurse in her hurry to leave after hearing about Saul and Jonathan's death. So, at five years old, an age when he should have been outside romping and playing with his playmates, he lost the use of both legs (2 Samuel 4:4). There was no electric wheelchair, none of the conveniences of this day, no grace—that is, until King David inquired of him (2 Samuel 9:4).

> Amazing Grace, how sweet the sound,
> That saved a wretch like me!
> How precious did that Grace appear
> The hour I first believed!

Grace, Grace, and More Grace!

Funny how grace shows up when it seems our legs have been knocked out from under us. Poor Mephibosheth! Even his name was a presage for his future. After all, *mephi* meant scattering, destroying, or contending (or fighting) with. The latter part of his name, *bosheth*, meant shame. Imagine having a name that always reminded you that you were fighting with shame. Every time someone called you,

you heard "fighting with shame." The shame of being crippled—of being disabled for life, the shame of being utterly defenseless. Have you been fighting with the shame of your past? The shame of imprisonment? Of sexual sin? Of lying? Of failed relationships? Of abuse? Grace gives us the power to overcome our evil tendencies through the power of the Holy Spirit. Grace gives us the ability not to retaliate when we've been mistreated. Grace enables us to humble ourselves, be quiet, and allow God to fight for us. All we need do is ask God.

And then one day King David ordered that Mephibosheth (the one fighting with shame) be brought from Lo Debar, the barren place, to a place where he would be shown kindness and mercy (grace). Have you been brought out of the barren place? Have you been shown kindness and mercy by the King?

The king's show of grace didn't stop with Mephibosheth. He showed it to his son, Mica, and to his entire household, including his servants. The Bible says Mephibosheth always ate at the king's table (2 Samuel 9:7–13). The point here is that God's amazing grace benefits not only the person to whom it is extended but also everyone in his or her immediate circle and beyond. Are you benefiting from grace shown to someone in your family, perhaps your mother, father, or grandmother? Endless ripples . . .

CHAPTER 19

Grace Is Personal

Grace Up Close and Personal

An examination of the word *grace* defines it as "unmerited favor of God toward fallen man." The wonderful thing about God's grace is that, even though undeserved, He still extends it to us. Isaiah 30:18 says, "Yet the Lord longs to be gracious to you; he rises to show you compassion." Imagine, the God of the universe longs to be gracious to us now!

Grace is personal, tailored to your life and mine. God metes out just the right amount of grace for each of us, based on our individual circumstances and situations.

Here's a personal example of what I mean:

In 2007 I was about to purchase a new home and thought I would be able to go to a local credit union service center to get a cashier's check for closing costs. Well, when I arrived there, I quickly found out that because the sum of money I needed was so large, I had to go all the way to the main office (about thirty miles away) to get the check and return to the title company. I had only a couple of hours to do it. Panic set in! I got on the expressway and drove like a professional race car driver. Imagine: I drove 91 miles per hour in a 70-mile-an-hour zone! I felt like I was floating over the road. Well, fifteen miles outside my destination, my float was cut short by flashing red-and-blue lights in the rearview mirror.

I braced myself for what I knew was going to be a lengthy scolding from the officer and a very costly speeding ticket. He looked like he was about nineteen years old. He leaned on the car and asked for license and registration, then asked me where I was going in such a big hurry. Suddenly I had a breathless attack of "run my mouth." I couldn't stop talking as I tried to explain to him I was on my way to the credit union in downtown Detroit to pick up a check for the down payment on my new condo. He let me blather on until I was near hyperventilation. Then he said, "Miss, you know something always goes wrong when you're closing on a house. The day my wife and I closed on our house, the car wouldn't start. We had to call the auto club to bring us a new battery! So, take a deep breath and calm down. Your closing isn't for two more hours." He issued me only a warning. No points were added to my license. My car insurance cost didn't go up. I closed on my home that afternoon. The most important lesson that came out of that incident was a wonderful illustration of God's amazing grace. The officer didn't know me. He had no reason to be kind and understanding. Driving twenty-one miles over the speed limit was clearly against the law.

- There was no excuse for my transgression. I was at the cop's mercy. I received God's grace.

Consider the following after you read Hebrews 4:4–6:

1. How many times have you knowingly transgressed God's commandments without thought of the consequences?
2. How many times has God been gracious toward you when you didn't deserve it?
3. When was the last time you extended grace to someone?

4. Has God ever taken a mess you created and turned it into a blessing? Describe the situation.

5. How did you feel when you looked back over the situation?

    Mercy is *not* receiving something we do deserve, and
    grace is receiving something we *don't* deserve. Grace
    makes endless ripples in every life it touches.

CHAPTER 20

His Grace Is Sufficient

But he said to me, "My grace is sufficient for you,
for my power is made perfect in weakness."
Therefore, I will boast all the more gladly about my
weaknesses, so that Christ's power may rest on me.
—2 Corinthians 12:9

I have spent a great deal of time over several decades ministering in the prison system on Sunday mornings. I can remember one morning when I woke up with a blinding sinus headache, and as life would have it, I was scheduled to bring the message that day. I had studied and prepared to deliver what God had given me, but I felt so debilitated by the headache that I didn't feel capable of delivering the sermon. Well, there were only two of us going, the psalmist, and the messenger, me. So, at five o'clock on a Sunday morning, I got on my knees and asked God to please take away the excruciating headache so I could deliver the word that day. As I knelt before Him, I heard the Holy Spirit say very quietly, "My grace is sufficient for you, for my power is made perfect in weakness." I immediately knew God had answered my prayer, but I didn't understand the answer. When I got up off my knees, I didn't feel any better; as a matter of fact, I probably felt worse. I wanted to crawl back in bed, but I was committed to serving that morning. So, I prepared myself and met my ministry partner at the designated place, and we made our way to the prison about an hour and a half away. That morning the Lord met us in the service. He spoke through my weakness and filled the altar with thirsty souls. I honestly don't recall when my sinus headache left, but it was gone by the time we completed our assignment. I was physically exhausted but spiritually exhilarated. I learned three very important lessons that day:

1. God uses weak people to demonstrate His awesome power (2 Corinthians 12:9).
2. We absolutely must rely on God for effectiveness in ministry and our everyday lives (2 Corinthians 1:9–10).
3. If Jesus Christ chose to depend on God the Father to empower His life and actions, what makes us think we can do anything for God by our natural abilities? (John 12:49).

Consider the following scriptures and provide your thoughts:

John 5:30

John 7:16

John 8:28

John 8:42

John 12:49

His strength is indeed made perfect in our weakness. We don't become strong enough for God to use. *Instead, we must become weak enough. God is strong in our weakness—that's grace!*

Light on the Word

Match the scripture with the following applicable statement about grace.

_____ Proverbs 3:34   a. Who has insulted the Spirit of grace.

_____ Romans 5:20   b. Where sin increased, grace increased.

_____ 1 Corinthians 15:10   c. He gives grace to the humble.

_____ Ephesians 2:5   d. Conversation be full of grace.

_____ Colossians 4:6   e. It is by grace you have been saved.

_____ Hebrews 4:6   f. But grow in grace and knowledge.

_____ 2 Peter 3:18   g. Find grace to help.

_____ Hebrews 10:29   h. The grace of God that was with me.

CHAPTER 21

Grace in the Pigsty

After he had spent everything, there was a severe
famine in the whole country, and he began to be in
need. So, he went and hired himself out to a citizen
of that country, who sent him to feed the pigs.
—Luke 15:14–15

We know the story of the prodigal son who was blessed to live a life of luxury with his father and brother. He had servants, fine clothing, and lots of money. By today's standards, he lived a movie star lifestyle, lacking nothing. One day he decided he wanted his share of his father's estate because it was time to strike out on his own. After all, what did his old man know?

So his father handed over the kid's inheritance, and he set out on his own. I'm sure he had lots of friends when he started. The hangers-on hung on until the money ran out. Then he found himself all alone. The redeeming factor in this entire story is in verse 17. "When he came to his senses and said, 'How many of my father's hired men have food to spare, and here I am starving to death! I will set out and go back to my father and say to him: Father, I have sinned against heaven and against you. I am no longer worthy to be called your son, make me like one of your hired men.'" So, in the middle of a pigsty, as smelly as he must have been, he decided to return to his father. Now, right here is where most of us would have decided we probably needed to clean ourselves up before going home. You're probably asking yourself, "What has all of this to do with grace?" Glad you asked! Grace says, "Come just like you are. Come with the stench of the world on you. Come with all your hang-ups, disappointments, misconceptions, brokenness, and hatreds." Whatever you do, just come!

The young son pushed past all his uncertainties about returning home, and scripture says, "While he was still a long way off, his father [grace] saw him and was filled with compassion for him; he ran to his son, threw his arms around him and kissed him" (Luke 15:20). The father didn't tell him to first take a bath, get a haircut, or put on some clean clothes. Grace just reached out, then embraced and kissed him—stench and all.

Light on the Word

Lilly came to church one Sunday morning and took up a seat on the front row, right smack in the middle. The charter pew members quickly removed themselves and sat two or three rows back or on the other side of the sanctuary. It became obvious from the aroma she emitted that Lilly hadn't had a decent bath in at least a month. Close observation of her gaunt and wrinkled face revealed dried spittle and tobacco around her mouth, and a mottled and filthy wig lay askew on her head. A glance at the members left no doubt about their discomfort with their uninvited guest. I distinctly recall observing the action from the soprano row of the choir stand. She didn't appear to be very old, probably in her late forties. She wasn't unattractive, just disheveled and filthy. As the service progressed, I noticed she began to get involved. She bowed her head during prayer and paid close attention during scripture reading. When devotional songs were sung, she clapped her hands and sang much too loudly. People in the congregation were so busy staring at her that they forgot to participate. Lilly had a wonderful time, though. After a while, one of the deacons tiptoed over to her and asked her to leave. I couldn't figure out why, since she was praising the Lord—what we were supposed to be doing. (I later found out she had been asked to leave because she smelled so bad.) For several months after that, Lilly came to the door leading to the sanctuary and stared through the little window. Someone taped paper over the glass to keep her from looking in. During this time, no one tried to get her cleaned up or to offer help. Grace took a sabbatical when Lilly showed up.

The Bible teaches, "As for you, you were dead in your transgressions and sins" (Ephesians 2:1). I rather appreciate the way Paul reminds the Ephesians (and us) of their past life of sin. I believe God put this scripture in the word because He knows we have tendencies toward spiritual amnesia. God knew we would forget when we were in our sins and didn't smell so good. "For it is by grace you have been saved, through faith—and this not from yourselves, it is the gift of God—not by works, so that no one can boast" (Ephesians 2:8–9).

Thinking back on Lilly, I wonder whether her filthy, disheveled appearance and stench weren't a reminder of our life before grace found us. Maybe we just forgot that Christ loved us when sin made us a stench in God's nostrils. Perhaps we forgot we were rescued so that we, in turn, could throw out the lifeline to another drowning soul.

Grace, and still more grace, that rescued my
ailing soul, And filled my heart with immeasurable
love, making my tattered life whole.

—LeVerta Massey

Consider the following questions:

1. What happens when we forget our past lives (before Christ)?
2. Based on Colossians 2:13, what was our old nature like?
3. What happened to the penalty for sin?
4. What then should our reaction be to individuals who need deliverance from sin?

Reflections and Prayer

For it is by *grace* you have been saved, through *faith*—
and this is not from yourselves, it is the *gift* of God.
—Ephesians 2:8 (emphasis added)

This humbles me because by nature I want to do something to deserve the deliverance that came to my life by way of Jesus's sacrificial death. I'm reminded of the old song line—"Not of good that I have done, nothing but the blood of Jesus!" Then I'm sobered by the thought that there has never been anything I could do that would be "good enough" to merit such a sacrifice. No matter how hard we try, we will *never* earn this marvelous grace. It is by *grace* we have been saved.

Father, in the name of Jesus, thank You for extending Your grace to this undeserving world. In our frailty, there isn't one thing we could have done to earn it. Thank You for choosing to love us and to give Your only Son on our behalf. We should be wearing the nail prints in our hands and feet, but Jesus bore them instead. Thank You, Jesus, for giving Your all! Amen.

NOTES

Book 1: Love Without Measure Is A Priceless Stone

Chapter 1: Page 9. 1 John 3:1; John 3:16; 1 John 4:21; **Page 11**. John 13:35

Chapter 2: Page 13. John 11:1–5; **Page 14**. John 11:7–8. **Page 15**. John 11:34–36. **Page 19**. Hebrews 4:15; **Page 20**. 1 John 4:18; 5:3; Where Love Is, Rev. Prof. Henry Drummond, 1851–1897

Chapter 3: Page 21. John 15:12–13.

Chapter 4: Page 25. 1 Corinthians 13:1–13; 16:14. **Page 29**. Matthew 5:46

Chapter 5: Page 31. 1 Corinthians 13:4. **Page 34**. 2 Peter 3:9b. **Page 35**. Psalm 90:4; 2 Peter 3:8–9; Hebrews 10:36–37. **Page 36**. Augustine's quote on love. **Page 37**. Matthew 18:23–34. **Page 38**. Matthew 18:26–30. **Page 43**. Exodus 20:6; Leviticus 19:18; Psalm 63:3; 130:7; Proverbs 3:11–12; 17:17; Matthew 22:37–39; 1 John 3:1

Book 2: Stripped, Beaten, and Half Dead: Compassion Is a Priceless Stone

Chapter 6: Page 46. Luke 10:30–37

Printed in the United States
By Bookmasters